# In the Moment
## Writing from a Spacious Mind

# In the Moment
## Writing from a Spacious Mind

A collection of poems & essays

Sylvia Duncan
Richard Fischer
Tina Lombardo
Sarah Muenks
Michael Pfeifer
Jennifer K. Sights
Mary Schanuel

**Spring Street Publishing**

**PUBLISHED BY SPRING STREET PUBLISHING**

Spring Street Publishing books may be purchased for educational, business or sales promotional use. For information, please write Spring Street Publishing, 7915 Big Bend Blvd., St. Louis MO 63119 or visit www.springstreetpublishing.com.

ISBN 978-0-6152-1566-2
FIRST EDITION

*Cover art by Tony Schanuel*
www.schanuelart.com

# Contents

## FORWARD
*Writing from a Spacious Mind*

This collection of poems and essays had its genesis in a small writing group that gathers every week after sitting meditation at the Missouri Zen Center in Webster Groves, Missouri.

First comes zazen, just sitting and breathing for 20 or 40 minutes. After bowing, with our minds more or less calm, the Zen Writing Group adjourns upstairs to the small library where the Zen of writing begins.

Each session, we take turns reading short pieces from Natalie Goldberg's *Writing Down The Bones* and *Thunder And Lightening*. We also read from Zen Master Dainen Katagiri's books of essays *You Have To Say Something* and *Returning To Silence*.

The selections are always random. We trust what we call 'bibliomancy,' simply opening a book to a random page. It doesn't matter if we've heard the passage before. Something new always takes place.

After each reading, we practice 'spontaneous writing' for seven minutes. Goldberg describes this practice in *Writing Down The Bones* and Julia Cameron suggests the process for writing 'morning pages' in her book *The Artist's Way*. Spontaneous writing also is similar to the automatic writing that surrealists practiced.

We put pen to paper and write continuously, without pause, following whatever the mind brings to the surface.

Having cleared the mind with Zen meditation, the unconscious is very near the surface. Sometimes the writing that follows takes a cue from the reading, as though a seed were planted. Other times, something completely different wells up.

Spelling, grammar, logic, style, form...none of those matter as we write, yet they appear in delightful ways as that which is inside of each person awakens.

Finally, we read to each other what we wrote, but make no critical judgment. There is no last minute editing. We accept what occurred at that particular moment just as we accept our experience in sitting zazen. Each breath is a moment. Each word is a moment.

This is where Zen and writing meet.

Zen is about simply sitting and awakening to being a fully alive human being, interconnected with the world.

Writing is about awakening the creative mind and allowing it to become fully alive and connected with the world.

In zazen, all thoughts are dismissed and allowed to pass through the mind and out into nothingness. In writing, thoughts are allowed to well up and express themselves.

In Zen writing, we turn off the tiny voice of the editor that lurks in our minds, the one that says "You can't say that! Who do you think you are? That's silly!" The editor is given the evening off and allowed to sink into nothingness.

The results of our writings vary widely. Even when we all write on the same subject, every person brings something different to the experience. Each evening is different.

The work presented here reflects some of those moments. These pieces have been edited only slightly – prose broken into lines of poetry, misspellings corrected. That is about the extent of the editing. What you will experience in reading this collection are those small moments in the library of the Missouri Zen Center.

Natalie Goldberg, by the way, was a natural choice as inspiration for our writing practice. Like us, Goldberg's writing often draws on the observations and discoveries of her Zen practice. Also, Goldberg studied at the Minneapolis Zen Center with Dainin Katagiri, who also transmitted the dharma to Rosan Yoshida, our *sensei* at the Missouri Center.

We offer our profound thanks to Rosan Yoshida, Dainin Katagiri, Natalie Goldberg, and Julia Cameron for the wisdom they have shared with us.

**Michael Pfeiffer**

## Amrita Unadumbrated
Rosan Daido

Friends, wherever whenever you are
Come and see the Way to Life!
When you sit solid and serene ever
You reunite with the source of life!

Take a step forward from the 100-foot pole.
Dive and drink amrita abundant, full
Filled with limitless life, light, love
Limitless liberation and law to save.

Your ideas are like clouds or water
Floating, flowing bound to nothing.
You become totally freed from all.
You become holy familiar with all.

The treasure houses open themselves.
The treasures reveal sacred selves.
You are breeze and you are flowers.
When butterflies fly, flowers bloom.

Drink amrita ambrosia inexhaustible.
Write amrita immortality indescribable
The liberated life, the miracle mind
Written on the life water with wind.

**Rosan Daido**
Missouri Zen Center
Dharma Heir of Zen Master Dainen Katagiri

am•ri•ta – a Sanskrit word that literally means 'without death'
and often refers to nectar or ambrosia

un•ad•um•brate – the opposite of adumbrate, which means to
cast a shadow over, shade or obscure

# NATURE

# Joy
Mike Pfeifer

Succulent secrets of evening,
Full moon just passing the tip of the tree.
What is required, except the joy of simple joy?
In complex times with many choices, the first choice
Must be to breath. Only when that is accomplished
Can we think of what is next.
Thus we sit and the moon waxes and wanes.
The sun appears in a clear, blue sky or hides
Its face in mist.
I hear the tiny frogs singing out of joy
For water and air and a few insects to eat.
How can I wish for more?
The air is filled with the sea
That rises and falls a thousand miles away.
It brings the scent of salt and memories of sweet scallops
Eaten while rain fell on the iron railings of an old balcony.
From here, the endless joy of living has been withered
More than once and sadness has fallen
Like the petals of a magnolia tree
As the leaves find themselves being born.

### Based
Sylvia Duncan

These hostas are enormous,
tall and wildly brave.
No drought will kill them.
They are well nurtured.
They have given birth here.
Some of their clan
were sold off.
They are a hardy group.

Breathe hostas.

I saw your Uncle
at the public garden.
He was tamed, quite tamed,
A venerable chap
with fine bluebell-shaped
wispy whiskers.
He leaned off to the side.
He would not conform
Until a gardener
staked him upright.

You, oh wilder ones
surround me.
Water plays your songs.

## Wild Mind Books Seen
Sylvia Duncan

Yellow custard sun
Not brassy or menacing
Ready for crayons
Ready for rays around it
Take it. Draw it.
Set it in a blue sky
With wavy one-stroke
Crayon birds.
Don't forget clouds around
Put in a row of
bulbous green trees
A house, a fence.
Take a deep breath. Sigh.
Sun wants to shine
Draw sun a family
a dog and cat.
Sun is satisfied.
It will move around
slowly all day
Knowing you have
Seen it.

## Joyful Leap
Sarah Muenks

Dolphins leaping joyfully out of the water! Their power, presence and beauty stirring the heart in mysterious ways as they allow our Spirits to Soar beyond the world of limitation!

Do dolphins get depressed? Their brains may or may not be more developed than a human's, yet they stir something in us that cannot be measured by science because it's real and eternal!

Dolphins may know sadness but I doubt they experience depression because they seem to relate from their Self, not their self. Depression arises outside of oneself, and I believe dolphins are relating from their Soul, their innermost core, as some humans do. Why is it that some people know joy while others feel a darkness that seems void of love?

The Soul, our Spirit, is like a dolphin, knowing moments of glorious passion while only the human mind is capable of creating a prison of depression. Our Soul is consciousness; thus it's leaping in exuberance and joy naturally!

**Voices**
Mike Pfeifer

Tzzzzzzz.
Cicadas.
Window glass like water.
The stream of sound.
Their echo is from the present.
Cicada. Groundling.
Struggling to climb and sing.
Tzzzzzzzz.
Cicada meditation.
Sound like a far wind.
A kind of knowledge
That cannot be heard.
Heard by not hearing.
This is the sound of the world.
The breath of grass.
The breath that exhales
Two dark birds into the sky,
Like two dark words fluttering around.
The tree they land in is like a razor.
Thin branches. Thin leaves.
The disappearance of something.
The disappearance of everything.
Disappeared back into this sound.
Lonesome, but sustaining.
Empty, but fulfilling.
It is the sound of one
Joined by many.
The chorus of trees.
The cicadas are their voices.

**Dandy Lions**
Jennifer K. Sights

The bunny sits amidst a field full of lions. He sits calmly, scenting the air, waiting. The lions wait as well. What a tasty snack, but nowhere near enough for all the lions there. What will the bunny do? Escape seems impossible, for he is surrounded by a dense sea of lions.

I look for signs of fear in the bunny, but there are none. So calm, accepting of whatever will come his way. Then the bunny looks up, a minute movement of his head. What does he hear, or smell?

Suddenly he takes off in a running bunny hop. The sea of lions takes flight as well, but not all follow the bunny. They scatter in every direction, floating up, down, left and right in a swirling whirlwind of white puffs. The bunny escapes unscathed, for it was not the King of the Jungle who surrounded him. He was in a field of harmless, white, fluffy dandelions!

But I suppose not everyone thinks dandelions are harmless. They spread their fluffy seeds and more flowers grow where they land. Though some call them weeds, killing them with harsh chemicals. My seven-year-old cousin thinks they are beautiful flowers. She gathers them from the yard and spends the day holding them to her nose, smelling their perfume. She sniffs them until her nose is stained yellow! Now there's a sight to see! Her yellow nose matches her blond hair, perhaps a shade darker.

One man's trash is another man's treasure. One gardener's weed is a little girl's flower. And Rachel had plenty of flowers Wednesday night after her dance recital, though none of them dandelions. Three large bouquets in crinkly cellophane; she could barely hold them all. And a beaming smile on her face, so excited. What a beautiful dancer.

7

## Night Falls
Mike Pfeifer

Night falls from day like a flower
And the darkening ground, the black dirt
Of the barren sky, accepts it.
In the falling there is an endless quality.
Night falls without ever reaching the bottom.
When does dusk end and night begin?
Who can point out the moment,
Sitting in the trees like a large bird?
When is night complete in itself,
Containing no light, no daytime, no unseen arc
Of light that has followed gravity and the earth's curve
To intrude silently and invisibly?
Day falls the same.
Dawn is just as intractable
And darkness too bends around the world
And enters where we never look for it
And so never see it.
These two are so intermingled
That they might as well be lovers
In each others arms in a happy embrace,
Embracing what cannot be embraced.

### Always There
Mary Schanuel

Grit and concrete
pigeon toes scrape steel
air thick with fumes
the breath of too many humans
breeze that blows sound
down the canyon of granite and glass
more colors than nature could imagine
all in one place
all guzzling gas.
A city.

Soft bubbling water
soap-shaped stones
tumbling stopping tumbling
tiny darting fish
moss that waves and dances
honeysuckle scented air
only my breath.
The woods.

In different moments
I visit each
and visit them both
in this moment.

Always there, despite me.

## Wind
Jennifer K. Sights

The wind blows through my hair
softly, peacefully.
I think what a wonderful world
ours must have once been
no air pollution
no noisy trucks
nothing but nature.
Life was simpler
long ago
no television
no computers
no electronics.
To truly enjoy
the simple everyday things
must have been
uplifting.
But that is gone.
Rush from place to place
hope that truck doesn't hit you
hope you live to see tomorrow.
Hope – is there hope left?
Yes. We can make hope
but only if we try.
Appreciate life
the sun
a butterfly
the wind
and you can have hope.

### Today's Truth
Mary Schanuel

I read today that the truth is in the details, that if you are going to write fiction, you must write it with as much truth as possible.

The knowing is in the familiarity, the commonness of describing something so well that a reader feels as if it were her own experience.

Here is today's truth.

The sun was too warm for January, and hidden behind blue--gray clouds at that, the kind that usually roll in on early spring afternoons.

I sat in my car for a few moments and caught my breath from the long day, or rather I allowed my breath to catch up with me. The breeze blew through the sycamore tree that had lost is leaves last fall and kicked up the rich, moldy smell of those leaves packed on the wet ground.

The air felt like Halloween. Thick, slow raindrops fell on my windshield and stuck there, with not enough momentum or passion to roll down the glass.

The moment was confusing.

What season did you say this was?

## Water Thought
Richard Fischer

Within me
  past the road of accusation
    past the Nazi of my righteousness
    past the little girl eating a banana
there is a white field of snow
  without a speck
  of dust or dirt or pollution
a field of clean cold frozen water crystals
  partying in the sun light
    taking the rays of photons
which can't decide
    whether they're wave or
             matter
  taking this
refracting it in
  myriad patterns of thought
  inhabiting the minds of men
  in a helter skelter jumble
  of twists and turns -
the snow flakes enjoy their play
  they want to commune
    with their fellow water drops
      held within the humans
    passing through those bodies
in order to get some idea
  what it is
  that happens in those
    bags of flesh
    where cells dwell.

## Prayer For The Lost Trees

Tina Lombardo

My affinity with trees began during childhood.
The kindly beings sharing our yard like Tolkien's Ents.
Generous providers of shade and breakers of wind
With deeply rooted feelings.

God, why did my father destroy
every tree we ever had
like a transmogrified Johnny Appleseed?
The plum tree – gone!
The mimosas – gone!
The ash tree and the two maples – gone!
We joke about it sometimes,
but what possessed the man
to take after those trees?
Why couldn't he accept and glide
like a summer breeze?
I'm searching for the bridge between me
and the lost trees.
Searching for renewal like the leaves
that come back every spring.

Waiting with a hopeful heart
an empty hopeful heart.

# What Needs To Be Done
Mike Pfeifer

What needs to be done?
The green shoots of jonquils
Need to push up through
Dark, wet earth.
Birds need to arrive
And announce themselves with song.
The clouds need to darken
And lower themselves
So that the sun may appear and disappear.
Whatever else happens, this must be done.
I need to see a bee, with its golden,
Brown, fuzzy body. The wind
Needs to take the last dry leaves
And the new growth needs to appear.
The redbuds need to cast an aura of purple
In the halls of the forest.
When these are done
More will ensue.
I will not be satisfied, nor will anyone else.
But what needs to be done will be done,
Making room for the perfection of every
moment.

## False Seasons
Tina Lombardo

We waited through the winter
long icy days.
Shivering in the blue air.
Spring came, bringing warm yellow relief,
punctured now by the air conditioning
of the office building.
Gagging me with remembrance of the cold.
Let me dress for the weather!
Loose clothing, sandals –
And leave the jackets in the closet
with the rest of winter.
Put away till next year,
like the blankets and the boots.

# CHANGE

## September
Tina Lombardo

September is here and I am happy.
A month of transition, of possibility, of change.
My favorite month.
What I really want to say is:
I am making progress overcoming fear and anxiety.
My children (loss of control)
My siblings (a see--saw of anger and love)
Ex--spouses (good god, won't they just cease to exist?)
My work (at odds with my art)
There, I said all that and my heart rate hasn't changed.
I am calm and unafraid.
I am in the moment more and more.
I am not easily tossed by people and events.
Not a tiny boat on a choppy sea.
I am the ocean.
I am September: in transition, changing colors,
ready to detach and sail down from the trees
held aloft on the air of change.
What I really want to say is:
It is September – and I am happy.

## Ode For The Floor
Mike Pfeifer

The wooden floor is a ripple
in the time of a tree
and the light, dimmed by paper,
is a wave of electric sun
struggling through the air
like a fish swimming in fast water.
I dream of a waterfall
that is only a slender thread of steel
surrounded by mist.
The thread seems substantial,
as if it could be climbed or taken
and beaten into forms
that would eventually become water again
and vanish from the wrist or the table
where they sat.
and there would be a faint roar
and the smallest movement of air
as the waterfall realized itself again
and plunged into its mercury shape
where the goddess once
strung it into a bow and a harp.

**Soothed**
Sylvia Duncan

She was wild-eyed. She would rush into the library when it opened and stay until we closed.

At five minutes to nine I would wake her. Her eyes were fierce and went from side to side like ping-pong balls. She had once told me that before she became an alcoholic she had been a registered nurse.

Her knitting was always in view on the table. I told her that I had learned to knit as a child. One day she was in a peculiar state of dementia, and as I passed her table she ranted.

"Those boys are tormenting me." I eyed the mischievous seventh grade boys and they quieted.

"I am here to knit." On and on she went until I asked her my magic phrase guaranteed to help me deal with any library situation.

"What is it you would like me to do?"

"Talk to me about what you knitted."

I could do that.

"I made socks," I said, "and once I made everyone I knew huge long scarves."

"Did they wear them?" she asked.

"My friend Barbara lost hers in the dentist's office and was distraught until she reclaimed it."

The woman liked this. It was a conversation. Just the two of us, the way it ought to be for a woman of the nursing profession who liked to knit.

The rowdy boys shuffled by, tamed by civility, tamed by talk of knitting, tamed by a new way of looking at the wild woman.

"What are you making?" I asked her.

## Difficult
Sylvia Duncan

The workshop was entitled "How to deal with difficult people." It was a three-day course for those working with the public. I came away with one sentence to use. It always worked, although it seemed impossibly naïve and simple – sappy indeed.

Difficult person approaches. Begins ranting. Asks to see manager. That was me.

"It's a CC," my assistant would murmur to me. CC stood for 'creates confusion.' It applied to the rowdy, the homeless, the graffiti artists who chased their peers through the public library branch.

"What is it you would like me to do?" I would ask.

When I first asked this, I imagined the responses to be that I should go to hell, or some similar phrase. But no, CC's always stopped, looked at me curiously and told me what they wanted me to do. If it were possible, I would quietly say, "I can do that for you."

If it were impossible I would shake my head sadly and say, "I can't possibly do that, but here is what I can do."

It always began with a redirection of their anger, a refocusing about what they expected of me. Sometimes a person would stop mid-rant to hear how silly their request actually was and would say, "I know you can't do this."

It only works with someone who is truly irate and disturbed.

## Against Travel
Mike Pfeifer

Don't travel.
Let the world come to you.
On storms.
On the dry wind of sunny days.
In the dark cloud of starlings
coming to roost for the night.
Let the world come to you
in the sad face of the woman
at the grocery store,
staring, perplexed,
at her shopping cart
which is nearly overflowing
with things she did not buy.
In the eyes of the child
just awakened
somewhere
across the city
and across the river,
who wakes to see
a flower in surprising bloom
Let the world come to you
in the breath of lovers
and in the gasp of their illumination.
Let the world come to you
in the breath of those who hate you,
even those who believe
they know the reason.
Let the world come to you
in the lazy spin of a cottonwood leaf.
Do not travel
or you will surely miss these things
and instead
rush into an empty room
with little light.

## Do It!
Sarah Muenks

Infinity is ever-present and our lives are beginning to
mirror, at deeper degrees, our Souls' highest intentions and
to express them in our daily existence. It is no longer
enough to be merely content or discontent, for those beliefs
are outdated because our essence is vibrating to a higher
calling, our true calling.

What may be my calling may not be yours – for only you
know what the whisper or roar of your Inner Voice is
saying. We cannot judge another's journey but we do know
what our own Soul is asking of us, what it is time to do, and
only I can act on that awareness.

Yes! Now! Patience and focus – both important qualities of
the quest but the time of action has arrived, arisen, been
birthed and this action is our heart song, our true calling
being revealed. DO IT!

## CHAOS – Notes For Kathy
Mary Schanuel

1. Chaos has its own order, and its own agenda.

2. Chaos knows what it wants for you and it will have it.

3. When you are in chaos, it is not your job to figure it out or sort it out or make it stop. You are not that powerful.

4. It *is* your job simply to feel what comes up in that swirling pot.

5. By feeling the feelings and moving through them, you clear the stones and logs, the walls and dark narrow boxes out of your own way.

6. So that chaos can do its work, take you to a place you could not have imagined going on your own.

*or, if you prefer less order….*

Chaos has its own order, and its own agenda. Chaos knows what it wants for you and it will have it. When you are in chaos, it is not your job to figure it out or sort it out or make it stop. You are not that powerful. It *is* your job simply to feel what comes up in that swirling pot. By feeling the feelings and moving through them, you clear the stones and logs, the walls and dark narrow boxes out of your own way. So that chaos can do its work, take you to a place you could not have imagined going on your own.

## Deep Dreams
Rick Fischer

Penetrate into your life
  from the outside
where you stand
  afraid of jumping
 off the edge
    of your doubts
  into the dawn of emptiness
where there is only the unfolding petals
    of your being
  ready to unveil
the jewel ornament of liberation
  hidden at the core
    filled with an inner light
  of truly freely madly deeply
abandoning all fearful holding onto
  any kind of pre-determinedness
  that might say "No"
    or "Hold on there"
      or "You better not"
  or some other kind of contraction
    that was left behind miles and ages ago
in another time and place
  before the true birth of You
    in the dawn of now, the real,
  the only one of all ones.

## Beyond
Rick Fischer

Beyond the usual,
  beyond the habitual,
    beyond the same thoughts
       day after day
    lies a vast field of fresh air,
   a fathomless deep ocean of living water,
a never ending expansion of time and space
  we call universe
    where all beings are interconnected
      in a matrix of give and take,
    a web of pandemillionific multiplicity
   ever regenerating new forms,
all connected
  to what has been and will be.
    Beyond the everyday
      is a world of undreamed of everydayness
    where new formations constantly evolve
   into free spirits
of body mind thought spirit
  beyond body,
    beyond mind,
      beyond thought,
       beyond any conceptualization
   of limited thought speak.

# ON WRITING

## Fresh Voices
Sarah Muenks

They met at the Zen Center. These authors with a fresh voice unique to the 21st century gathered, all knowing there was a reason they met. Was it the talent, the camaraderie or did they all glimpse the place in history they were in and would create?

They each had their unique style of writing which was evident in their published works. But there was also a common thread in their writing, their lives, their connection that kept them meeting Wednesday night, week after week.

Future generations will say, "Oh, if I could have been at the Zen Center – my life, my destiny would have been fulfilled! To be in one room with those brilliant writers!"

The Professor will agree but will also look the student directly in the eye and say, "Now it's your turn to write, to publish, to let out your fresh voice, thus creating your own Sacred Legacy as the Zen Writers did!"

## You Can't Do It Alone
Tina Lombardo

We write in a group.
We never tear each other down.
We bolster each other and find a way
to appreciate every word.

Each secret piece of remembered or imagined joy
or sadness – or humor.
We are held together by our love of words.
Writer's group.
I tell anyone who asks,
"I write with a group on Wednesday nights."
It defines me.
broadens me
leads me
sustains me.

I eat it up and spin it out like silk
on these yellow pages.
Even when I'm empty and there is nothing to say
I'm here writing.
Maybe something will come of it.
Maybe nothing.
Regardless, I continue to write
about everything that happens
and things that never will.

## Poet's Prayer
Tina Lombardo

We could read these poems all night
and never grow tired of the words.
Each one, a beacon, shining light into the shadows.
broken by the morning sun,
but always waiting to engulf us again,
leaving us with fragile candles of hope.
And these poems.
Emerging like singular stars
in an endless sky of ink.
delivering warmth and meaning
to punctuate the darkness with brilliant strands
for us to cling to
while we drift
astride a huge wave of compassion.
or is it fear?
It's neither one. It's something else.
A longing for more
than the ties that secure us.
The loosening of the ropes.
The freeing of the mind.
These poems exist because we need them to.
Without them we are lost.
No direction.
No true north.
So read and write
To save your soul.
Amen.

## I Am A Writer
Tina Lombardo

Writing is big and brave and dangerous.
When I sit at the table with my cup and carafe
and put the next blank page in front of me
I am up on the high dive preparing to jump
Will I tell the truth? Yes, I will.
The truth that comes out of my pen
as it moves across the page.
My wild mind is engaged and I let it go.
I'm alone except for the cat and the dog.
What do they think I'm doing?
Can they tell this is different from the other things I do?
Sometimes I play music. Sometimes it is quiet.
I jump and plunge into the depths of my mind, my
memory, and my imagination.
The other activities in my life begin to pale because
I am a writer.
And I can write whatever I please.
I don't have to let anyone read it.
Or maybe I will.
It's not about the agent or the publisher or the movie deal
or the Pulitzer.
Not when I'm sitting at this table.
It's about me and the page.
Me and the high dive.
It's about the spring of the board,
the jump, the splash,
the immersion, the depth.

I am a writer.

## So What???
Sarah Muenks

I write because I have to. It springs forth from the core of my being, and when the time has come for an idea to be born into this reality, nothing can hold it back.

I realized the other day that I absolutely love to write! I always have. It's an arena where I again push the envelope past what I've seen to work into that mysterious place writers know, that place that allows words to form, to create, to be. A place of silence.

Silence, like writing, is raw and pure! In creating a novel, I love to go to a place where I've never been and write a story I've never read, in a style unique to what is being told.

I guess I also live life the way I write – outside the box. My life is guided more from an inner wisdom than from outer information. The strangest words to me have always been, "Well, that's the way it has always been done."

So what??? We are here on this glorious and challenging planet to walk to our own beat and be true to ourselves – then we will be true to our writing and our writing will continue to reveal to us the deeper mysteries of life.

## Doubt
Sylvia Duncan

Why doesn't doubt visit me? I need a little doubt.

Here doubt! Come here. Come shake your shaggy ears my
way. I will grasp them, pull them, and scoff at you right
there. Merrily I churn out all of the accumulated
information I have stored. There is no room for that old
doubt.

I see him at my students' doors. I coax them on admiringly,
as doubt slides by their chairs.

"Look, write another paragraph," I urge them. "This one
will not be quite enough for you. It is a launching pad, a lily
pad in a large pond of doubt."

That is why I want to meet doubt, tell him off, shake him,
send him along without a meal from me or my small army
of writers.

If unfed, he will not return. I see him as a puffy, staid
invader. He rattles his heavy chains.

That's right, come closer. You and I will wrestle. I will win.

# WILDNESS

## Wednesday in Montana
Tina Lombardo

The rainbow rides the ranges.
I follow in its colored tracks.
Out here I feel your eyes without looking.
Out here we touch as if searching.
I am gone into the jagged peaks of the
mountains.
I lay my spine across them and shape the
horizon
With my thoughts.
They will echo at twilight
In the sunset
When the rainbow goes to sleep
To paint dreams.

## Brow
Sylvia Duncan

A see-through brain would come
With a remote control
Set on the brow
Tiny as the tiniest of cell phones.

Click
Click on happiness
Tired of grinning
Click
Click on serious
Ten clicks for sleep channel
Mustn't make that too easy.

Click somber for funerals
Click merry for weddings
Click four times
For creativity
Keep it there on that channel.

## Heart Strings
Rick Fischer

heart flow down
 into the labyrinth
  of cool blood red corpuscles
  oxygen
    with electrons flowing around a center
        somewhere
      in the minus power
        of quark consciousness
    willy nillying into and out of
        you me you me weeeee
vibrating into reality with interconnection
   reflecting the red flow of awareness
        into cells that want to be touched
          by blue
    the open blue of light
  in the spectrum of visibility
        where actual potential
                    transformed
    into a baby's breath of awareness
      seizes on the sound
    of beat beat heat
        feet are for fleeing
                    into the unknown present
 of new possibility
        without pretense of anything
   winging into yes
now I will just do it
        if only the witness will allow
    the openness to penetrate
      fear of what
        am I afraid of anyway

## Pegasus Dreams

Jennifer K. Sights

Horses, graceful horses dance through my dreams, carrying me away to a world of endless spring, endless sunshine, rain showers of honey sweet on my tongue. Laughing, tinkling bells, children playing, dogs running, barking. I leap onto my horse's back and ride, ride, ride.

"When will you remember freedom?" the horse asks. "This is freedom," I reply. Freedom to run, to laugh, to dream, to fly. To fly?

Suddenly we lift into the air, flying towards freedom, towards dreams. Dreaming of horses, dreaming of nothingness. The world is black. It is blue, purple, green, a rainbow of colors.

A girl child walks on the rainbow of life, skipping along beside her pony. A magnificent mare protecting them on the journey. Sparking pure white mare from a fairy tale. I join them on the path, but am not ready for the truth.

## Trees Dreaming
Richard Fischer

Trees rustle in expectation
    of the coming rain
   stretching their limbs in a Pilates exercise
    of pre-rain anticipation
  dreaming lives of humans
   who continue to think
     they are their own lives
unaware they are actually
 dreams of trees –
    rooted in the earth,
   connected to the rhythms
of minerals and fungi,
    slower organic movers and shakers.
Trees sense the movement of clouds
    bringing oceans of moisture
      in huge sky waves over vast distance,
   relaying the atmospheric internet
    of evaporation respiration
  where far east is just around the corner
    intimately connected with the arctic
      and vast dry Sahara
 trees in their connection
    direct the dream lives of the two-legged ones
providing in their oxygenic exhalation
     the precursors of the dreams that fill
   the subconscious of the two-leggeds
    with the psychic direction they need –
the two-leggeds are not yet awake
  and need this direction.
They hope, one day, two-leggeds will awaken
  and begin to communicate the full
     inter-species extra terrestrial symphony
 of evolutionary cooperation
      going on for millennia.
   Trees are patient.
   They have eons.

## Infinite Expression
Sarah Muenks

Wild Things! Wild Life!

Going past the safety of the norm, feeling that wild, raw,
uncontrolled part let loose within and the wild fire of
writing pour out.

I love traveling for the wildness it brings
my days as a student in Madrid
sitting in the cafes
hiking in the mountains
Paris one weekend
the Southern beaches of Portugal the next
stories and adventures that could fill volumes.

Our recent trip to the Upper Peninsula of Michigan comes
to mind. The beauty and ruggedness of that Sacred land
and the untamed waters that beat against its shore are still
vivid to me. I can still taste the delicious pastie, a local
delight, which Tom and I discovered in a cozy café in
Houghton.

Now another wilderness is calling – it is a story to be
written which is unknown to me at this moment. I have felt
the wildness of a writer, the pure raw energy that lets loose
when a story must be told, that place where there are no
boundaries, judgments or separations
only one life, one heart that we are all a part of
the beating
the passion
the joy
the dance of knowing
there is only One Mind expressing itself
in Infinite Expressions!

### Predator
Mary Schanuel

Black lava flows up from
somewhere
I don't know where
it comes from but it must be hot
a place where I can't breath
where the air itself is red and thick.

I carry a cold black lava stone
deep in my heart
lodged so comfortably
that I usually don't notice it's there.

Sometimes I feel the predator
rise in me and instinctively
I move with it
snarl and snap my teeth.

When I step back for a moment
I am aware that my heart
is not all soft and warm.

This cold blackness is there
where the predator lives.
This unfinished grief lashes out
moving to protect
the raw, vulnerable place
that never heals.

Then I take a deep breath
the stone settles back
into its place
and I forget again
that it is there.

## The Space Between
Rick Fischer

The space between the awareness
 and the thought,
the emptiness between an object
 and its conception,
the freedom between the urge
 and the denial,
the warmth between the feeling
 and the smile
these moments call to one's authentic wholeness
 urging a reassessment of the habitual pattern
and presenting the possibility of independence,
 the option of creating something original,
the chance of being true.
 The path taken creates a universe at odds
with that which was not chosen,
 but freedom always opens a new door
into a path of growth.
 The path not taken lives its own life
in the myriad worlds of some physicist
 daydreaming on the stool in a john
off the mile diameter accelerator
 under a wheat field in Illinois.

## Prairie Fire
Mary Schanuel

The animal in me is a mouse
hiding in a soft dirt burrow
beneath a dry prairie
cozy with the worms and rolly bugs and fleas
totally unaware of the grass fire
that burns just inches away
all around the tunnel hole.

Fire smolders
close to the ground
mostly unseen
until a sudden breeze gives it life
breathes energy and pure oxygen
into its heart
so it dances and leaps and flares
changing everything once again
into the stuff we're all made of
ash and dust
steam and energy.

I am the mouse. I am the fire.
I am the grass. I am the breeze.

# ZEN

## An Idea In Your Mind
Tina Lombardo

An idea in your mind floats like a puffy white cloud in the
blue firmament.
Or a balloon full of helium with a dangling string
attached to nothing
floating free.
Sailing higher and higher through stratospheric
levels of consciousness
until the air changes,
bursting the balloon,
helium flowing out
in tiny molecules.

Now where is the idea? Is it hiding?
No. Look! There are more balloons.
New colors.
Floating.

The idea in your mind is big.
So big you can't see it.
It surrounds you with words and sensations and pockets of
silent awareness.

The idea in your mind is a dream when you sleep.
It carries you through sunshine and singing
and happiness and space

Punctuated by another idea in your mind.

## Laughing At The Rice Cake
Tina Lombardo

It's a painting of a rice cake – a sesame rice cake.
A painting of a nice cake – from long ago.

It's the answer to a riddle – a Dogen diddle diddle.
A Buddhist with a fiddle – from long ago.

It's the blue and the green of the mountain and the sky.
The amber flecked gold of the mud in your eye.

It's a tiny silken eyelash – fallen on your cheek.
And a heavy book with footnotes – like musical feet.

It's the color of the truth when you breathe a long sigh.
It's the turn of your head when you whisper goodbye.

It's the laughter of the children – their hunger satisfied.
As they gobble down a rice cake
A painting of a rice cake
The colors of the rice cake
Nice cake
Pie!

## Open Heart Compassion
Jennifer K. Sights

If I can open my heart
Feel compassion for all
I can spread peace throughout the world.
Peace to me, peace to those I love
peace even to those I hate.
This sounds so simple, so refreshing, so pure.
Then why is it so hard?
Why can I not open my heart?
I feel anger, sorrow, pain.
Why can I not let go,
find the well of compassion
I know is deep inside me?
Why can I not open my heart
and find the peace, we all so desperately need?
Open my mind to the joy of emptiness and acceptance.
See the world from a different view.
It is not all about me.
Other people have feelings, thoughts.
I must accept other people
In their goodness and imperfection.
I must even learn to forgive
those who have caused me pain.
Only then will I be truly open.
When I can feel compassion for
and love all beings
only then can my heart be truly open.
Open to the limitless possibilities
that this beautiful world has to offer.
Open to see the beauty around me
to truly see it, appreciate it
not just in the closed mind view
I have today, seeing but not knowing
the intricate connection between all life.
Knowing that all beings are connected
I must have compassion for all.

**Bodhisattvas Come Out Of The Woodwork**
Mike Pfeifer

Bodhisattvas come out
    of the woodwork.
They stand in line
    at the grocery store.
They walk behind an ox
    in a rice field.
Maybe they bend down
    to pick up a leaf
From where it has fallen.

## Hunter
Sylvia Duncan

Arrows point and show.
Arrows are decisive.
They know which way is up.

If an eye with a paintbrush,
a marker or chalk
draws arrows on your path
Hop forwards and backwards.
Hop here, hop there.
Don't stop to stare.
Keep your eye on the arrows
Move straight ahead,
sideways or backwards.
Keep in your head
the direction of arrows.

If you feel it is clearly
the way for you
Hop quickly, or slowly
Keep moving.
Wait.

If your head says
these arrows mislead
Step back to your own
Game of hopscotch. Hop. Hop.

## Rounds

Tina Lombardo

OK – When we were children we sang rounds. I'm astounded to think about that now. The coordination it took for one group to start and continue singing while the second group came in at just the right moment. Then the third group began and for a while all three groups sang in unison then gradually dropped off, one by one, until the final group finished.

Why only three groups? Why not endless, limitless, groups joining in at just the right moment for a round that goes on forever?

Row Row Row your boat. Gently down the stream. Merrily Merrily Merrily Merrily. Life is but a dream. A dream. A dream

**Dogen's Dream**
Mike Pfeifer

A lake of a thousand yards was how Dogen saw himself.
The tranquil surface and a fish swimming to the bottom,
like the confused mind, singing and searching everywhere.
The tranquil light of the brilliant moon recalls the mind
awakened to it's self and not self, awakened to lake and fish,
to water and moon. The cryptic master I picture, sitting
beside a lake where a stream flows in, ever disappearing
into the blue depths. The melting snow of the mountains
sings as water and in the summer cicadas join the chorus.
All these fade into silence that is as subtle as the first breath
drawn upon waking, in the moment before consciousness,
when a purity of purpose and mind are all that exist
between the slanting sun and the dark room. And the sheets
are cool from a night of repose.

## Arrogance
Mike Pfeifer

Time is arrogance.
It assumes it flows,
Or we assume it flows.
It has no meaning really,
Except what we give it in 60 segments,
Per some unit, per some unit.
It should all stand still for a moment
And then drift gently to earth,
Like Buddha's flower petal.
The petal is small and velvety
And yet none of us can lift it
From its place or take it back
To where it once was.
It is, in this moment,
As solid as a mountain.
The flower mountain
From which the world suspends itself,
Holding disbelief and dropping it
Into an ever flowing stream.

## The Snowflake Path
Mike Pfeifer

The snowflake is the returning stream.
The stream is the returning snow.
The mountain is with them both.
It is the height from which the snow descends;
The height from which the stream descends.
Descending is only another way to rise.
Rising, the sun enters the cold air
And illuminates the mist, the mist which has risen
And accumulated in the low places overnight
To now twist up through the trees
And hold the sun for a moment.
It burns off, but the mist remains and the sun remains.
This is a comfort, because everything is leaving,
Escaping from this moment.
Plunging headlong into the next.
This is how I know I am falling.
Because everything else is falling with me.
It seems motionless, but casting an eye
Beyond these thing I can see the rush
Of the stream, the path of the snowflake

## 100 Foot Poles

Rick Fischer

The hundred-foot pole calls out to you.
   "Come darling, try out my new adventure!"
Everyday they appear
     in the front yard,
at the grocery store,
     on the side of the highway,
calling like sirens,
 and Ulysses,
     lashed to the mast of your life,
feverishly yearns for release
     to climb and jump,
to jump and fly (or die).
Lately the 100-foot poles
have been popping up,
         everywhere,
         in the Senate,
         at the White House,
         in Osama's garden,
         all over California,
they're calling for everyone, everywhere
wake up,
     wake up,
         pick up your sleeping mat,
rejoin the living
     in the world of October,
the world of evening lives
where all you have to do is
     take one small step,
         one step of infinite grace.

# Black Dog Of Emptiness
Rick Fischer

The black dog of emptiness
lifted his leg
and released pent-up fluids
        on my life
    invigorating the casual indecisions
with a fertilizing odor
            of change,
and then to compound things
he hunched down and
    laid a big warm dollop
        of perplexity
    into the flow of the events
haunting me
    with questions of
what if
    the night sky stars
            are speaking secrets,
what if
    OZ is simply on the other side
                of my mind,
what if
    the cicadas steer the sun
            through galaxy
                    with their song,
    and question upon question
        of alternate realities
                offering endless opportunities
        if only I will awaken
    to the lumbering gate
            of a wagging tail
ready to wag me into
        a new way of being –
    the wagging fortune of black emptiness
        humming contentedly.

58

## A Twilight Zone Moment
Sarah Muenks

A twilight zone moment may have happened. Did I miss it or did it miss me? Maybe I'm eating only M & Ms and I don't even know it because I've convinced myself that our different labels for food are correct.

A Twilight Zone moment may be continuously occurring.

I think I'm awake now but the moment may approach that has me waking up and waking up to what? I look around and what I thought isn't – what I knew isn't. I ask how can this be happening? Suddenly I realize that the world I am awakening to is real!

I take a deep breath and walk into this world and nothing I define is accurate so I give up definition, and then I begin to experience everything in the moment FULLY. In this strange but wondrous place the sounds are pure or am I really hearing for the first time? The tastes – OHHHH, I'm really tasting! The colors are so vibrant!

Then I realize I'm where I've always been but haven't fully experienced until now. I want to STAY AWAKE and not go back to sleep! And I know the only way to stay awake is to BE completely present NOW!

## Zen Mind
Mary Schanuel

Sitting.

I imagine that my mind, a bank of clouds, occasionally
parts, letting the blue sky and yellow light of creativity flow
through.

And then I realize I am 'doing thinking' and the clouds
close right over.

I picture a cloth, a piece of silk, sat upon for so many years
that the threads have shifted in places, leaving gaps where
the light, the One light, can come through.

But that recalls a sieve, and now my thoughts tumble
through, uncollected.

I am trying to find a way that my mind can go still and let
the moment pour in.

But caught up in the trying, I realize
a moment too late
that the bird has
just stopped
singing.

# MOMENTS

### thank you e.e.
Tina Lombardo

e.e. cummings you've got me humming.
i'll croon in june while staring at the moon
and thank all the gods for summer time tunes
and childhood games like making clover chains
then run indoors escaping the rain.
and crowding round our favorite board game
while raindrops encourage the flowers to grow.
we listen to the sound of cackling dice
the tick tick tick of little cars like mice
one space at a time round and round we go.
no need of clocks on days like these
just our friends and our games
and the afternoon breeze.
how rare these summer days would seem
reflected through the hazy screen
of time and tedious groan up games.
not like the warm puddles
where our piggies used wriggle.
deeper waters now and
oops!

## Johnny Apple Juice
Rick Fischer

Picking up the drinking glass
    with cows walking around
        the outside surface,
cubes of ice inside
    in the remaining apple juice,
        frost fogging up the clear glass,
picking it up – ice tinkling, juice jostling,
    upstairs the women revel in secret camaraderie,
        laughing the laughter of conspirators,
    on the front porch Tenmo
        wanders back and forth pasturing the flock,
the apple juice flows into my mouth
    down my throat
        sweet and sour and vinegary
bellowing the song of Johnny,
    the crunchy apple song,
        the song of ripe redness.

## Kindergarten
Mary Schanuel

I didn't go to kindergarten. My mother had five children and 'six-year-old' was her favorite age. So she kept each of us home for that year, since kindergarten wasn't required.

I'm sure I benefited from the extra time to watch clouds turn into fuzzy animals and follow ant trails across the porch. But that year at home put a huge dent in my early social life.

When I arrived at first grade, I was the only one in the class who didn't know someone else – a terrifying experience.

One morning early in my school career, I got my shoes muddy at recess and had to stay back to clean them. As I scraped the clay off my Buster Browns, I saw half a dozen first-grade faces leaning out the window of our classroom, and they were laughing at *me*.

"Mary got her shoes muddy! Mary got her shoes muddy!" they sang out.

I panicked and ran for home – an entire mile. I didn't stop until I got to the big intersection at Main Street and the Belt Line, where I had to push the crossing button and run alone across four lanes of waiting traffic.

My little seven-year-old heart was pounding hard as I finally snuck a look back, certain that a nun in her black, bat-like robes was after me.

But no one came.

I made it all the way home, apparently before anyone noticed I was gone. That, perhaps, was the even greater insult.

I was so afraid my parents, especially my Dad, would be angry with me for running away. Instead, my father gave me a lesson I would never forgot.

When he came home that morning, after having a pointed discussion with Sister Marie Something-or-Other, he told me that the nuns were wrong for letting me go home alone.

My Dad said the nuns were in charge of the school and that I should respect their authority, but that I should always question authority, too.

I always have.

## Center of the World
Rick Fischer

The precise center of the world
lies at the moment
          you look out the window
  facing southwest on the 81st floor
      of the south tower
          of the World Trade Center
  and see a large airplane
heading right at you.
After a few moments of disbelief
    there is a short eternity to drop
      the mountain of unimportant things,
              to see that you are
            going on a new journey
      right quickly,
    and to make amends and forgive
          all the silly little faults of yourself
          and everyone else
    before you move on
        to that new
              appointment.

## Beast On My Path
Mary Schanuel

One cold morning, I was walking down a snowy mountain path in Wyoming and came upon a moose.

We both stopped, startled, and stared at each other. I felt my skin go warm and prickly as my heart raced and adrenalin pumped through my body.

The moose was enormous, but that doesn't begin to describe his sheer animal presence. This close up, I could see his matted brown fur, some of it bleached red by the sun, some thin where he had rubbed his itchy hide against a pine tree.

Across this brief expanse of still snow, I could hear his throaty, snoring kind of breathing. I could see a dew of breath on his whiskers, sparkling in the thin winter sunlight.

He considered me for a moment, sizing up my less-than-impressive presence. He chewed his jaw back and forth once, then again, as if he were making a judgment call. Expend the energy required to bolt. Or not.

He decided against it, dropped his mouth to the snow and sucked in a bit of moisture. Then he unceremoniously lumbered off.

Once I recovered from the stunned sensation, I realized something. Unlike the moose, I hadn't even considered bolting, mesmerized as I was by the presence of this beast on my path.

## Darkness and Light
Jennifer K. Sights

I look at the black menacing sky,
the clouds hovering over
look like the teeth of a demon.
No light comes from the fright that is the sky.
The wind picks up and blows the clouds aside,
revealing the face of the goddess,
her shining beauty lighting
a bright path through the otherwise dark sky
that is the road for so many.
I bow to the moon,
thanking her for her gift of light.
I give thanks to the goddess for this night.
Though clouds fill the sky, hiding the stars' light,
it is beautiful still. Nothing,
nothing but the moon and clouds
filling the sky. They wait expectantly,
but for what? For the coming of a great being?
For the silence this world so rarely gives?
Does the moon wait for her lover,
the one she can never be with?
Or is it something more? Something I will never see,
never understand until I pass into their world,
the world of darkness and light together.
Or will I never know why she waits?
Will I always be unsatisfied?

## Down Below
Mary Schanuel

The town of Montepulciano is a walled village atop a steep hill in the region of Tuscany.

Our apartment was tucked into the highest corner next to the wall, where pigeons roost and swallows soar each evening.

The owners gave us directions to the *duomo* below, the cathedral that sits majestic in the golden sun at the base of the hill.

"*Sotto, sotto, sotto.* Down, down, down," they said.

And so we took that road, past the three cats in the brick alleyway, past the milk bottle tied to a fence post, down past an Italian gentleman tending his December garden, tying up a small twig trellis with his daydreams of peas, past the fresh green sprouts of artichokes, still six months from their warm, golden harvest, down past new celery and a few tiny green tomatoes still clinging to brown vines.

He offered no response to our *buon giorno* as we tramped by, gravity pulling our feet and legs *sotto, sotto, sotto.*

## The Joy
Tina Lombardo

Behind the resentment is the joy.
The laughter
The light
The cheer
The love
The feeling
Free-wheeling
No kneeling
Or stealing
But lots of dizzy reeling for joy.
Pure joy.

Behind the resentment is the joy
Giving warmth
Remembrance
Generosity
Big smiles
Kindness
And grace.
Shining joy.
Burning joy
Breeze of joy
Blowing fear and anger
away.

Refreshing
Rejuvenating
Invigorating
Effervescent
Nose tickling
Joy.

Pass it on.

# PASSAGES

## Magical
Sylvia Duncan

A young, very slender girl with features as sharp as a hawk's leaned on the glass display counter at her kiosk. Her wares were very expensive sunglasses. I watched as my friend was lured in to the shiny displays.

The salesgirl transferred her knowledge about those glasses in a few sentences. She had memorized many phrases about the superb lens, the comfort of the frames, the protection of the eyes against sun damage.

"You deserve the best," she insisted, and added more information.

"You only have one pair of eyes so take good care of them," she scolded.

She showed my friend a little case for the sunglasses, then produced a quaintly packaged square of cleaning silk.

"What color is your favorite, amber or emerald? You choose," she murmured.

The final amount was totaled.

The glasses sat on my friend's nose as she pranced down the mall. Without promotion they were nothing, just another pair of glasses. But with promotion, with knowledge of all of their properties, they were magical.

## Feel
Sylvia Duncan

I had childish artistic ambitions in a somber adult mind
that day. I intended to make a sympathy card for a friend
whose mother had died. I took the art materials, gathered
up another sketching friend, and we marched briskly to the
rose garden.

"I'll draw or paint her a rose," I said, business-like. "Then
I'll think of some suitable words. I have my calligraphy
pen."

There I was on the stone bench, pencil in hand, when a red
rose leaned in to touch my elbow.

I looked around. A dying, faded gold rose dropped petals at
my feet. My friend was busy, head bent. A whole art class,
some twenty students with enough gear to paint a cathedral
ceiling, were headed for the lilies.

Technique. I needed technique before I could draw this
rose. I had words. I needed to get closer to the roses. I
wanted all the words ever spoken, all the lines ever drawn
to say, "I am sorry about your loss."

I began to draw with tongue hanging out of my mouth, like
the ten-year-old I had become. I was able to feel the rose.

## Cemetery
Jennifer K. Sights

Cemetery. Peaceful and quiet.
Those once in our lives resting.
Still in the afterlife.
Does our presence disturb them?
Perhaps. Perhaps not.
I think not…or so I hope.
Quiet contemplation.
Soft conversation.
Safety among those passed.
No harm here. Only quiet.
Safety in your arms.
Comfort. Calm. Serenity.
I never expected to find
among the dead.
But why not?
They are at rest.
We are, in a way, at rest as well.
A new feeling.
Feeling of love.
Feeling of belonging.
Accepted by all around us.
Those who no longer speak.
Not as we do, that is.
The serenity of this place,
the calm of the moment.
Moonlight shining down.
All feels right.
All is good.
Have I finally found
what I so dearly need?
Acceptance found in the peace
of a quiet, moonlit cemetery.

## Nothing
Sylvia Duncan

He had a cure for insomnia.
Nothing exciting, he said.
He patiently explained it
To someone who was mortally ill.
Think of nothing. Say *nothing*
Spell the word *nothing*.
She tried it. It worked well.
She was asleep in five minutes
Of nothingness.

The next day she told me this.
I would rather be awake all night
In pain, feeling the pain
Than feel dead while I am still alive.

I tried it myself – the nothing method –
One night after I swigged three coffees
Watched a lurid film and suffered
From itching eyes
On rumpled sheets.

Toss, toss toss.
I knew what the word toss meant then.

Nothing. I said *'nothing nothing nothing.'*
Delicious heavy eyes and sleep
Dead while alive? No. It was a feeling of
Shifting into neutral
Getting out of a wrong gear
Into the absurdly benign nothing.

## Token
Tina Lombardo

I still have that white handkerchief.
I keep it in the pocket of my good coat.
The one I wear in winter when I go to plays with my sister.

I keep it handy so I can wipe away the tears
when I'm touched by the actors on stage
as they try to convey something
to a room of expectant faces.
Their courage is overwhelming.

The handkerchief was given to me by my first husband.
He pulled it from his pocket as the final scene of *Sophie's Choice* played out in front of us in the darkened theater.
I was sobbing loudly
with tears streaming and nose running.
I put the handkerchief to good use.
It met the flow of my emotion.

It was our anniversary.
Our first night out since the birth of our second child.
Afterward we drove straight home to our babies without
even stopping for a drink or a bite.

I still have the handkerchief.

## Memory

Tina Lombardo

A ring of stones in an open field
defined by moonlight.
The darkness glistens all around us
and smiles the mysterious night away.
Within the circle, safely moored,
Holding the sadness of our wisdom,
we sit, trying not to strive.
The slippery night slides us through the snares
Of the moment.
The rocks remind us of our closeness.
Thank you blessed night,
Whose god is a garden of stars.
Thank you for the memory.

# Jump
Jennifer K. Sights

I stand at the base of the mountain, looking up. I breathe in deeply, exhale slowly, and repeat. When I am calm I begin the climb up the side of the cliff. Hand over hand, foot above foot. I take each step slowly, mindfully. Finally, I reach the top. I can see all around me for countless miles. An eagle soars in the distance, hunting for food for the babies I see in the nest across the ravine. Small animals scurry away from my approaching footsteps. I see all there is to see, but still long for more. What else is there up here? Is there more for me? I step to the edge of the cliff and look over to the lake below. It's not that far. I know people have jumped and survived before. Why can't I? I take several deep breaths, contemplating the water below. I take the final step towards the edge, and then…

## It Starts With A Red Tulip
Tina Lombardo

It starts with a red tulip on a big round white ceramic bowl.
My mother's potato salad bowl. That's what the bowl was
for. Mom's potato salad. She used to bring it to the Chain
of Rocks amusement park where we had our school picnic,
back when we were in elementary school. Lots of lovely
tulips on that old bowl.

We marched from the grade school to the park, the whole
student body, kindergarten through sixth grade. I marched
with the baton twirlers from 4th grade on. Our music
teacher trained the twirlers. The infinite patience that
woman must have had. The baton was an instrument of
power and beauty and grace. One white tip larger than the
other. I twirled it and bounced it off the ground, catching it
with one hand.

Years later – adulthood. Traveling with a friend to Kansas
City for a business meeting. We stopped at the Apple
Wagon antique store on the way. Rows and rows and
shelves and shelves of stuff. There on the high shelf it
caught my eye. The companion piece. White ceramic
cookie jar with red tulips, circa 1950.  Did I buy it? You're
damn right I did.

## The Wall
Mary Schanuel

When I first saw the Vietnam Wall in Washington, DC., I was disappointed, like seeing a movie after reading too many glowing reviews.

I'd heard about The Wall for decades, seen photos of daisies and notes stuck into the cracks next to loved ones' names. I expected to feel the palpable loss hanging low like a heavy, damp mist in that small, shadowed valley.

Instead, it was a bright spring day. Most of the visitors were young, in their twenties. The names listed on The Wall could have been their uncles, even grandfathers, but not their brothers or high school friends.

At first, I didn't understand The Wall at all. My rational mind wanted direction, explanation.

Why were the names in odd alphabetical order, arranged in small groups, not A to Z from one end to the other?

Why were the first panels so short and the center ones much taller, full of so many names? Why did the panels taper down again to just a few? What did it mean?

And then I understood.

Each panel represented one day in the war, and the names of men and a few women whose breath flew out of their bodies one final time that day. The loyal soldiers who had died together were listed together, from A to Z. Some panels displayed just one name. Others listed an entire platoon of soldiers.

I stood amongst the tallest of the slabs and looked up, the sky blue and white above me. I continued on to the end and finally traced my finger across the very last name on the very last panel.

How sad, how very tragic, I thought, that *this* man had to die too, after all those many others lost before him.

## Heart Secret
Rick Fischer

The secret in your heart
    is there but not there,
  visible but unseen,
    open but not clear,
      clear but invisible,
visible but camouflaged
  by all of the things we learned
    that we didn't really need to know
because we learned them incorrectly
  from other blind seekers.

The secret is everywhere,
  written on blades of grass,
    leaves of trees,
      openness of skies;
written on water by the breeze,
    whispered by mice in pantries,
      spoken by squeaks in stairs,
and we do not see them
  because we are looking for anything
      but them,
anything but what we really are.

The secrets still call out to us
    to taste
      their sweet juiciness
        and smell their scent.

## Deliriously Happy
Sarah Muenks

I had one of those Deliriously Happy (D-Happy) moments lately. Monday night Tom and I had a date night. We went over to Stir Crazy and created our own stir-fry and talked and relaxed and connected. There was something unearthly about the evening. There was a peace that transcended time, a magic, a love that connected us.

Then we walked over to the movie theatre to see a flick. We realized it had been ages since we had watched a movie or rented a video. The theatre was almost empty which was magical in itself and I found the movie both entertaining and hilarious – or was it simply I was so D-Happy?!

We returned home and the peace was still present! This peace, this feeling was so profound because it was like experiencing something that was not of this earth AND it remained into the night AND continued into the next day! It is not present as I write but in a way it is because I feel it!

## Vision
Sarah Muenks

I had a vision when Tom and I were in San Francisco
visiting some friends. We were all walking in Tom's
sanctuary – Muir Woods – amongst the giant Redwoods. It
was breathtaking, magical and mystical all in one.

Tom was so excited to share this Sacred place with me!
And once we were there we felt such peace surrounded by
these ancient trees.

Then when Tom was walking in front of me I suddenly saw
Joe, our son-to-be, walking behind his dad (Tom) in his
hiking boots, jeans and wearing a small backpack. This
beautiful and radiating boy was so happy to be hiking with
us on this Sacred Land. For a moment, linear time ceased
because I felt the reality, purity and gift of being with Joe
and Tom in such a beautiful place!

## Once In the Sixties
Tina Lombardo

There was a young man with bushy red hair, who went by the name of Cheetah. I learned much later that his name was actually Ken, but that name didn't fit him at all. And another young man, big, tall, and gentle, called himself Hugo, though his name was really Paul.

One night we stayed up so late with our friends that the light changed many times. We had walked through several doors of perception, as people will do when they are spending time with chums called Cheetah and Hugo. We were sitting by the windows at the front of the apartment when a sound reached our ears from the street below. It sounded like a huge wheezing creature making its way slowly up the street toward us.

We were fascinated and a little alarmed. We cautiously pulled the curtain back and looked out the window to see what on earth it could be, coming closer and closer.

"It's the stweet sweeper!" said Cheetah.

So it was. What a bizarre creature that stweet sweeper was. Hugo laughed and said "I tell you, it's not the dope you smoke. It's the people you smoke it with."

Morning was turning the black sky to grey. Gradually the auditory hallucinations diminished and we crawled off to sleep until it was time for the first class of the day.

## Heart Bursts
Sarah Muenks

What makes my heart sing?
So much that it takes my breath away
to even ponder such a thing!

I look at the full moon
and my heart bursts with JOY!

I awoke this morning to ice
glistening outside my window
only later to see
the first yellow bud of the season
signaling spring
and all the color it will bring.

I feel blessed with the gift of life
with my loving husband,
our home and the marriage
we are creating one conscious step at a time.

I am grateful when I connect with another
living the song of the heart,
for it further ignites my own passionate
and totally unpredictable creative fire.

We open up to each other
knowing that what we say
will not be judged
but embraced and understood
as we travel along the road
of Living one's Dream!

## AUTHOR BIOGRAPHIES

**Sylvia Duncan** spent her first 24 years in England. She was born in a tiny village and has never shaken off her love of bluebells, violets, primroses and medieval words. She teaches, writes, tells stories and has published in many genres, including St. Louis newspapers where she occasionally rants in a humorous manner. She co-authored a children's book and some storyboards with Richard Fischer. She was a featured storyteller at the 1992 St. Louis Storytelling Festival. Her pastimes include swimming laps and playing Scrabble.

**Richard Fischer** grew up in the wild lands in the center of America near the big mounds and down river from the land of the mythic Huck where he was taught abstraction skills in the educational institutions of the later 20th century. He was adopted by the Muse at an early age and has enjoyed the works of his Muse siblings in this and other ages. He enjoys the connection he feels when he becomes one with the flow of word music. His Zen fellows assure him that it is akin to Buddha talk.

**Tina Lombardo** continues to seek the path of right action in the Midwestern USA. Her goals include letting go, waking up, and living a Bodhisattva life. She intends to complete her third novel this year.

**Sarah Muenks'** writing reflects her passion as well as the spirituality that guides her daily life. She loved growing up in Michigan in a close family with her parents, brother and sister. She also attended college in Michigan and studied abroad in Madrid, Spain. She currently resides in St. Louis, Missouri with her husband Tom, whom she married in a Sacred Ceremony in 2002. She is blessed with four SoulKids, two grandsons and close friends who create her La Familia in St. Louis. Her mother was a brilliant and creative editor and assisted Sarah in editing these essays. Sarah has finished a memoir on the passing of her parents and the LOVE that keeps them connected!

**Michael Pfeifer**, born in St. Louis, Missouri, received his M.F.A. in poetry from The University of Iowa's Writer's Workshop in 1980. He also earned a Bachelor's in journalism and a Master's in English from the University of Missouri – Columbia. He won the 1987 "Poet Lore" Ratner-Ferber Award and his poems have appeared in numerous small magazines. He lives in Kansas City, Missouri. Besides Zen, he likes Macintosh computers, cats, seashells, blackberry cobbler and thunderstorms.

**Mary Schanuel** has been a writer since she could hold a pencil, and has published fiction, non-fiction, entertainment reviews and poetry since she was 18. She compiled and edited the book *Animal Crackers And Alphabet Soup*, a collection of family humor written by her mother, Micky Mueller. Mary's writing has appeared in regional and national publications including *Working Mother Magazine, Organic Gardening,* the *Los Angeles Daily News, The Heartbeat* and *LifeSherpa*. She and her husband Tony have three brilliant daughters and three beautiful grandchildren. Mary is deeply entrenched in her first novel.

**Jennifer K. Sights** has been writing for as long as she can remember. She has completed her first young adult novel and is working on a second. She loves reading and writing all genres, and cannot see herself writing for just one. She lives in St. Louis, Missouri with Tiberius, her black Lab mix.

**SPRING STREET PUBLISHING**

Spring Street Publishing books may be purchased for educational, business or sales promotional use. For information, please write Spring Street Publishing, 7915 Big Bend Blvd., St. Louis MO 63119 or visit www.springstreetpublishing.com.
ISBN 978--0--6152--1566--2